UNCLE SAM'S KIDS

WHEN DUTY CALLS

Written by Angela Sportelli-Rehak
Illustrated by Gregg Hinlicky

AN ABIDENME BOOK

Copyright 2002
Abidenme Books
Post Office Box 144
Island Heights, New Jersey 08732-0144 USA

First Printing, 2002
Second Printing, 2003
Third Printing, 2003
Fourth Printing, 2004

Printed in the United States of America

Publisher's Cataloging-in-Publication Data Sportelli-Rehak, Angela. Uncle Sam's kids : when duty calls / written by Angela Sportelli-Rehak ; illustrated by Gregg Hinlicky.
-- 1st ed.
p. cm.
SUMMARY: Three children discover Daddy will leave on deployment. They learn fun ways to deal with separation anxiety and show they care while Dad is gone.
Audience: Grades K-4.

1. Children of military personnel--Juvenile fiction. 2. Separation anxiety in children--Juvenile fiction. 3. United States--Armed Forces--Military life--Juvenile fiction. [1. Children of military personnel--Fiction. 2. Separation anxiety--Fiction. 3. United States--Armed Forces--Military life--Fiction.] I. Title

PZ7.S76386Unc 2002 [E]
QBI33-867

LCCN 2002093905
ISBN 0-9714515-1-6

Dedication

For Nicholas, Breana, Micaela and all of Uncle Sam's Kids,
May God bless you and keep you in the palm of His hands.
You are truly America's unsung heroes and to you I remain
"Semper Fi"

Pat you will always be my shining star...

“Listen up Troop 109 ,” said Mr. Flagstaff. “Our country needs you!”

“Cool,” said Nick, “What do they need us for?”

“We must do our share,” he said. “Uncle Sam's Kids have been asked to be in a special contest. It's called ‘How to Show You Care When Duty Calls.’ The troop that comes up with the best idea to show their family and friends how much they care while they’re out at sea, will win a tour on a huge ship. It's called the USS Liberty Bell!”

M'S KIDS OOP 109

Nick thought of a farewell party that was thrown for the Cammy family by some of their friends. Sergeant Cammy sang songs and juggled a spoon on the tip of his nose. It was a happy night. Nick had a warm, fuzzy feeling as he remembered being with others, telling jokes and sharing stories. He knew he and his friends could think of lots of fun ways to show how much they care and give away that same warm feeling he had that night.

USK
USK
109

After school, Nick ran all the way home from the bus stop. When he got to the front door, he almost ran into it, but Daddy blocked it. He jumped up and down and dropped his book bag on Dad's big toe.

"Oow!" shouted Daddy.

"Sorry," gasped Nick, "but guess what? If all of us in the Uncle Sam's Kids club win this contest, we get to go on the USS Liberty Bell!"

U

“Wow, that's great,” said Daddy, with a jolly laugh.

“The USS Liberty Bell is a really big ship that can carry lots of airplanes. It's called an aircraft carrier.”

“Have you been on it?” asked Nick.

“No, but I will be, for about six months.”

“Huh?” groaned Nick.

“Well,” said Daddy, “Our unit has been called on a deployment and six months is how long we'll be out at sea.”

SK

“Daddy, what's a deployment?” asked Nick's little sister Breezy, who was coming down the stairs.

“A deployment is when sailors or marines just like me go to other countries to work for a while.”

Breezy looked worried and asked, “Daddy, does this mean that when you're not here, we won't be a family?” she cried.

“Oh, no honey. No matter where I am in the world, we will always be a family, because all of you live with me in my heart.”

"You are Uncle Sam's Kids," said Daddy.
"We have an Uncle Sam?" asked Breezy.
"No, Uncle Sam is the name of the character who stands for all of the people in the United States."
"Oh, I get it," she said.
Mommy then walked in on Daddy talking and added, "even though the hardest part of Daddy's job is being apart from all of us, we have a tough job too."
"What's our job?" asked Lil'M, the baby sister.
"It is to stand united as one big family while Daddy's called to duty," she said.
They all smiled and felt better.

Later on that month, Petty Officer Spangle went to the Uncle Sam's Kids' award ceremony at Nick's school. She stood tall and spoke clearly.

"I'm sure everyone did their best," she said, "but this year's winners of the 'How to Show You Care When Duty Calls' contest is Troop 109! Let's hear it for their great idea, the Care Sackpack! They used imagination and teamwork to send special packages to their family and friends, filled with goodies and treats to remind them of being at home."

All the troops clapped and stomped their feet.

Nick couldn't wait to get home and tell his family the great news! When he got there, he ran into the house and shouted,

“Mom, Mom, our troop won. We won the contest! Now we will all get to go and tour the USS Liberty Bell with Dad!”

“Wow,” exclaimed Mommy, “Way to go! I am so proud of you!”

POW

The big day was here, and the whole family got out of bed that morning before the sun came up.

"Ready to go?" asked Daddy.

"Yes, sir," beamed Nick.

"C'mon, after breakfast you and I can put my bags in the car," he said.

ROCK
Zap

Petty Officer Spangle greeted everyone at the ship.
"Welcome aboard the USS Liberty Bell," she said. "Our first stop is where the controls are kept. It's called the bridge. Single file, the steps up to the bridge are small."

"Next stop is the berthing area," she declared.
"Wow, is this where the babies are born?" asked Lil'M.
"No, there are no babies on the ship. This is just where the sailors and marines sleep."

"Carry on scouts," she said with a grin. "It's now time to visit the flightdeck. All the jets and helicopters take off and land on top of it. Watch your step as you climb down the steep ladderwell."

"The last stop is the mess hall. This part of the ship is where the sailors and marines eat their meals." Nick looked at his buddy and snickered, "If we eat here, it will definitely be a mess hall." Then, Petty Officer Spangle glanced at her watch and announced with a smile, "It's almost noon. Let's get lunch!"

After lunch, Petty Officer Spangle handed a merit badge to all of the kid's in Troop 109, and read them this special letter:

Dear Uncle Sam's Kids of Troop 109,

I would like to salute all of you, and thank you for your ideas.
All of us at Old Glory Base are proud of each of you.
Your troop has been a great support to all
the families of the sailors on the USS Liberty Bell, and we hope
you show them how much you care while they're deployed.

Semper Fi
Colonel Redglare,
Commanding Officer
Old Glory Base

Dear Uncle Sam's Kids of Troop 109,
I would like to salute each of you for all your helpful
All of us at Old Glory Base are proud of each of
Your troop has been a great support to all the
families of the sailors on the USS Liberty Bell.
Keep up the great work.
Semper Fi
Colonel Redglare
Commanding Officer
Old Glory National Guard Base

The time came for Daddy to deploy. He pulled out a jar with a yellow ribbon wrapped around it. It was filled with red, white and blue candy stars.

"You three are my superstars," he said.

"Is that why you gave us a jar filled with candy stars?" asked Breezy.

Daddy smiled and said, "That's right, honey. The stars are a reminder that I will be home with each of you as soon as I can. Each night before you say your bedtime prayers, I want you to look out your window and wish upon the brightest star you can find. When you find it, eat a piece of candy. Wherever I am, I'll be wishing on the same bright star, and I'll remember that each night you eat one is a day closer to me coming home!"

Breezy gave Daddy a tight squeeze around his tummy, and Lil'M gave him one around his leg. Daddy picked them both up and said, "Lil'M, draw me lots of pictures at kindergarten. Breezy, you practice your first grade penmanship."

Then he smiled a great big smile at Nick and said, "You keep up all your great work with the Uncle Sam's Kids Club. I'll call you as soon as I can. I love you all." Then he gave each one of them a kiss.

Everyone waved their flags as they watched him walk onto the ship.

After only a few days, Lil'M started crying, “Mommy, I miss Daddy.”

“I got it!” said Nick. “We can make Dad a Care Sackpack. It was that idea that helped our troop win.”

“That sounds great!” said Mommy.

Lil'M then smiled and chimed in, “Yeah, let's send him bubble gum.”

“And cookies too,” shrieked Breezy. Mommy added some of her own stuff, then put all the goodies in a big brown box to bring to the post office.

SUPER
Semper Fi

Time passed, and it was now the week before Christmas. Nick read an e-mail he printed out from Dad:

Dear Nick, Breezy, and Lil'M,

I miss you all so much. The Santa Claus cookies were delicious, but the star cookies ruled. I am so excited because the holidays are here, and when they pass, spring will follow, and soon I will be home! Give Mommy a kiss.

Love, Daddy
xoxo

Spring was here at last, and Daddy would soon be home! The next two weeks were busy. Everyone met at the Old Glory Base to make signs and banners for the big homecoming of the USS Liberty Bell. “Mr. Flagstaff, look at our banner,” said Breezy, “we painted it in red, white and blue and used one of Mom’s old sheets!” Mr. Flagstaff chuckled, “Looks great, I’m sure your mom will love that you used one of her old sheets!”

come
e Daddy

The big day was here! It was here!

“Mommy,” yelled Lil'M, “Look! Look! All the candy stars are gone! Daddy's coming home!”

Everyone got dressed so fast that morning.

They couldn't wait to pick up Daddy at the docks.

Mommy was so happy. “Get in the car,” she said, “and don't forget your flags!”

ddy

It was Daddy! Daddy was finally home! Mommy, Nick, Breezy, and Lil'M ran to greet him with lots of hugs and kisses. Lil'M jumped into his arms and giggled. “Daddy, now that you're home, all the candy stars are gone!”
He smiled and said, “That's the best news I've heard in a long time!”
“But why?” asked Lil'M, with a puzzled look on her face.
Then Daddy said, “because at last, when I say my bedtime prayers, I no longer have to search the sky to find the brightest stars. You're all right here with me!”

DAD

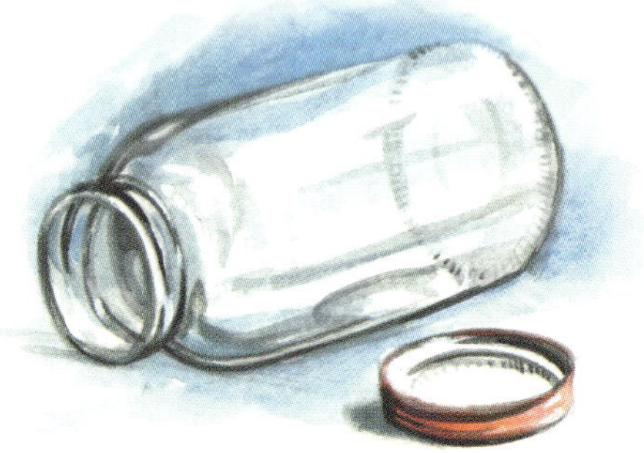

There are 50 hidden stars throughout this book,
one for each great state.
Now go back and take a look,
count them, don't you wait!